ILLUSTRATIONS, AND PHOTOGRAPHS // BY KINNIE STARR

First edition.

House of Parlance Media, Inc.
202–1636 West 2nd Avenue
Vancouver, British Columbia
Canada V6J 1H4
www.houseofparlance.com

Library and Archives Canada Cataloguing in Publication
Starr, Kinnie, 1969-
How I learned to run / Kinnie Starr
Poems.
ISBN 978-0-9738131-3-5

I. Title.
PS8637.T367H69 2008 C811'.6
C2008-902200-9

Editor: Billeh Nickerson
Copyeditor: Tonya Martin
Cover design: Ingrid Paulson
Interior design: Mauve Pagé

Printed in Canada by Webcom
10 9 8 7 6 5 4 3 2 1

Canada Council for the Arts / Conseil des Arts du Canada

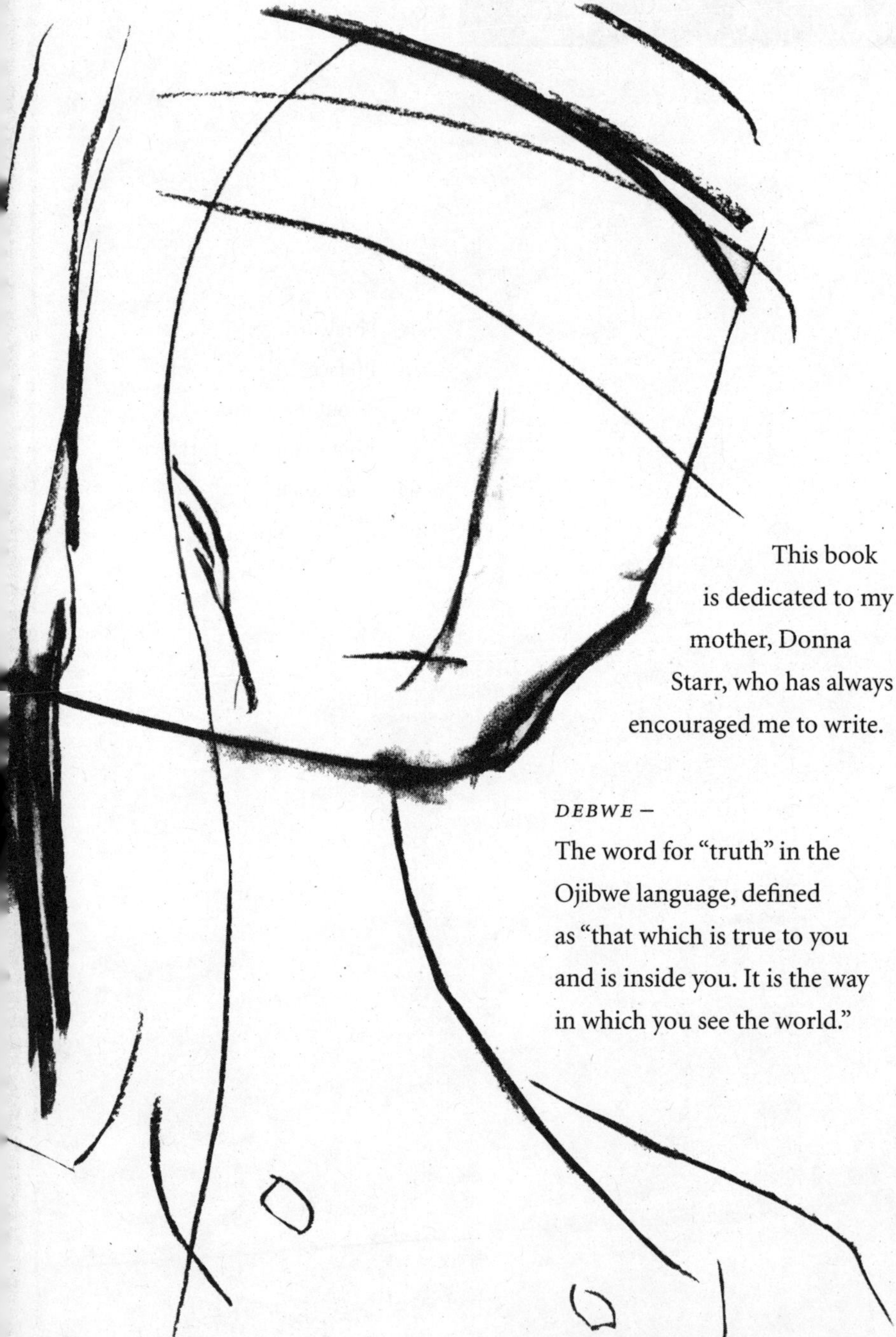

This book
is dedicated to my
mother, Donna
Starr, who has always
encouraged me to write.

DEBWE –
The word for "truth" in the
Ojibwe language, defined
as "that which is true to you
and is inside you. It is the way
in which you see the world."

TABLE OF CONTENTS

FOREWORD

There are rhythms and beats in every movement that is made by an artist. These patterns ripple like brave waves on a clear pond. The effects vibrate through the earth and move up through the soles of our feet to journey through our bodies, whispering stories of our history. The patterns of struggle, rhythms of survival and beats of resilience surround us — our families, and our communities as we continue to walk on this land.

There hasn't been an indigenous female musician who so clearly spells out the experience of our nation's cultural history, oppression and genocide as eloquently. As audiences hum and traipse along to her spoken word beats or folksy acoustic rhythms, most don't realize they were just given a history lesson. Kinnie Starr does just that. She does it in a way that allows her audience to share her experience and her ideas. Once touched by her music we come away with a stronger sense of what we are fighting for, what we are holding onto, and what we are trying to remember.

In her first book, Kinnie delivers more than beats and rhythms. She recites to us as if we were walking with her by the lake. It's intimate and powerful. We are given an opportunity to understand Kinnie's relationship to the Indigenous cosmology — which her ancestors speak through her — by the way she experiences the world and tells us her story. We experience her evolution: from a woman yearning to belong; to sexuality fruition; to becoming the teacher she always sought; to the strong woman she has become. Emotional and painful, inquisitive, and laugh-out-loud funny, by the end of the book Starr's ripples become torrents in the cultural pond.

Harmony Rice, Publisher, *Spirit* magazine

PREFACE

Over the last ten years of making albums and touring all over the world, I have been asked hundreds of times if I have a book of my poetry available. Here is that book. It is a collection of unpublished writings, drawings, and photographs.

I would like to thank Shane Koyczan for recommending me to House of Parlance as a writer worth publishing. I would like to thank Cathy Barrett and Sandy Garossino, Billeh Nickerson, Stuart Pierre and Jay Daunheimer, Ingrid Paulson and Mauve Pagé, and Mandy Wheelwright, Paul Seesaquasis and Canada Council for the Arts for helping this book come to life.

A GOOD TRAIL

If you find a good trail follow it/ That path will become your own / For the rocks resting underneath your feet / And for the fire on your tired face /// For the wind that trails your pant leg / And for the poison that falls down your throat / For the shadows you know to be your own / For this and more you

will never be alone /// For the kiss misfit upon your lips / And for the hands that broke your child body / For the words you wish you had spoken / And for the sadness that weakens your bones / For your long walk looking for home / For this and more you will never be alone /// For the tree is your spine, see? / And those are blessings you cast everyday / That is your voice and voice is power / And these are winter's burdening hours /// That is the seethi

hing of clever hidden fears/ And these are times you rest to shed tears / That is the future you see in your reflection / It is the coming of new generations /// It is the truth that we all know/ It is the guide even silence bows down to/ She slows to the beat of each heart / For this we pray and play truth's part /// For the tree is our spine, see? / And this is truth that we now speak / The time has come that we must meet / For those are rocks that rest underneath our feet/ These are the shadows we know to be

If you find a good trail follow it
That path will become your own
For the rocks resting underneath your feet
And for the fire on your tired face

For the wind that trails your pant leg
And for the poison that falls down your throat
For the shadows you know to be your own
For this and more you will never be alone

For the kiss misfit upon your lips
And for the hands that broke your child body
For the words you wish you had spoken
And for the sadness that weakens your bones
For your long walk looking for home
For this and more you will never be alone

For the tree is your spine, see?
And those are blessings you cast every day
That is your voice and voice is power
And these are winter's burdening hours

That is the seething of clever hidden fears
And these are times you rest to shed tears
That is the future you see in your reflection
It is the coming of new generations

It is the truth that we all know
It is the guide even silence bows down to
She slows to the beat of each heart
For this we pray and play truth's part

For the tree is our spine, see?
And this is truth that we now speak
The time has come that we must meet
For those are rocks that rest underneath our feet
These are the shadows we know to be our own
And what is more it is a long walk home
It is a long walk home

our own / And what is more it is a long walk home / It is a long walk home

A LAKE

On my surface   I am boats   Roaring engines   Teenagers driven   By anxious pace   With burnt face

I stare down the sun   Unaware of *race*   Of grandparents   The spill of gasoline   *This stain upon me*

At my centre

I am your clean lake

Deep water

Full of quiet history

Lost legends

My arms are weeds

Indigenous

They grow

Toward you now

Thin as sun rays

Strong as time

COVERED BY YOU

I cover myself in you • In the smell of your skin • I adore your rough patches

You poke and prod yourself • Throughout your days • With fingers under

I wish I could surround you • With the way I see you • I would

• Dark lips • Eyes on fire • Smile bigger than the moon

• Pale and elegant fingernails

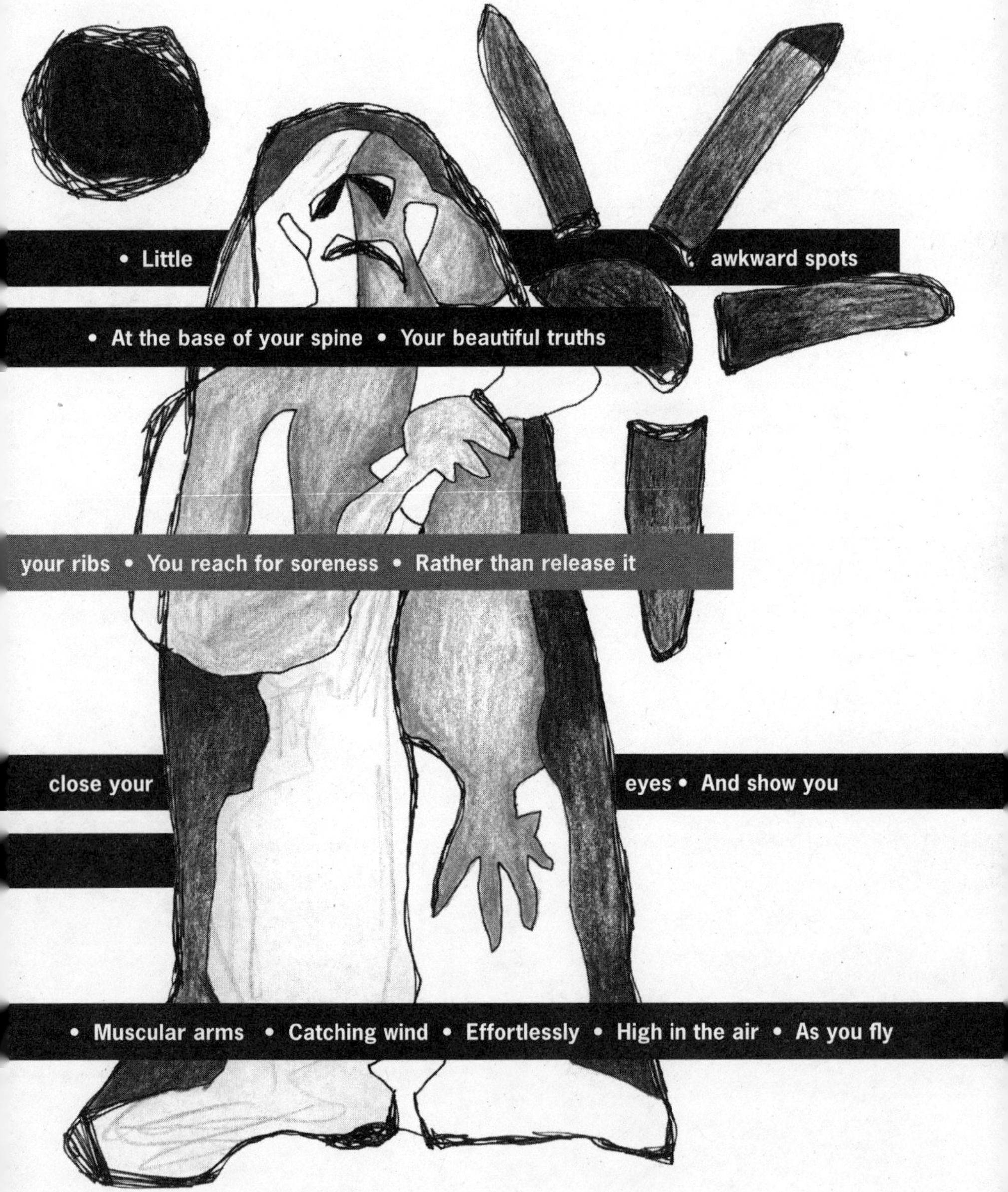
• Little
awkward spots
• At the base of your spine • Your beautiful truths
your ribs • You reach for soreness • Rather than release it
close your
eyes • And show you
• Muscular arms • Catching wind • Effortlessly • High in the air • As you fly

EVERY INCH

Look at me
Like you used to
Like I am a mystery
See me
Really rest your eyes on me
Like you have never seen
My beauty

Lay your hands on me
But hesitantly
Like you used to
Wide-eyed
You marveled
At my sharp small waist
Deer legs
Comic-book proportions

Feel me
Like you used to
Before you had access to
Every inch of me

YOURS

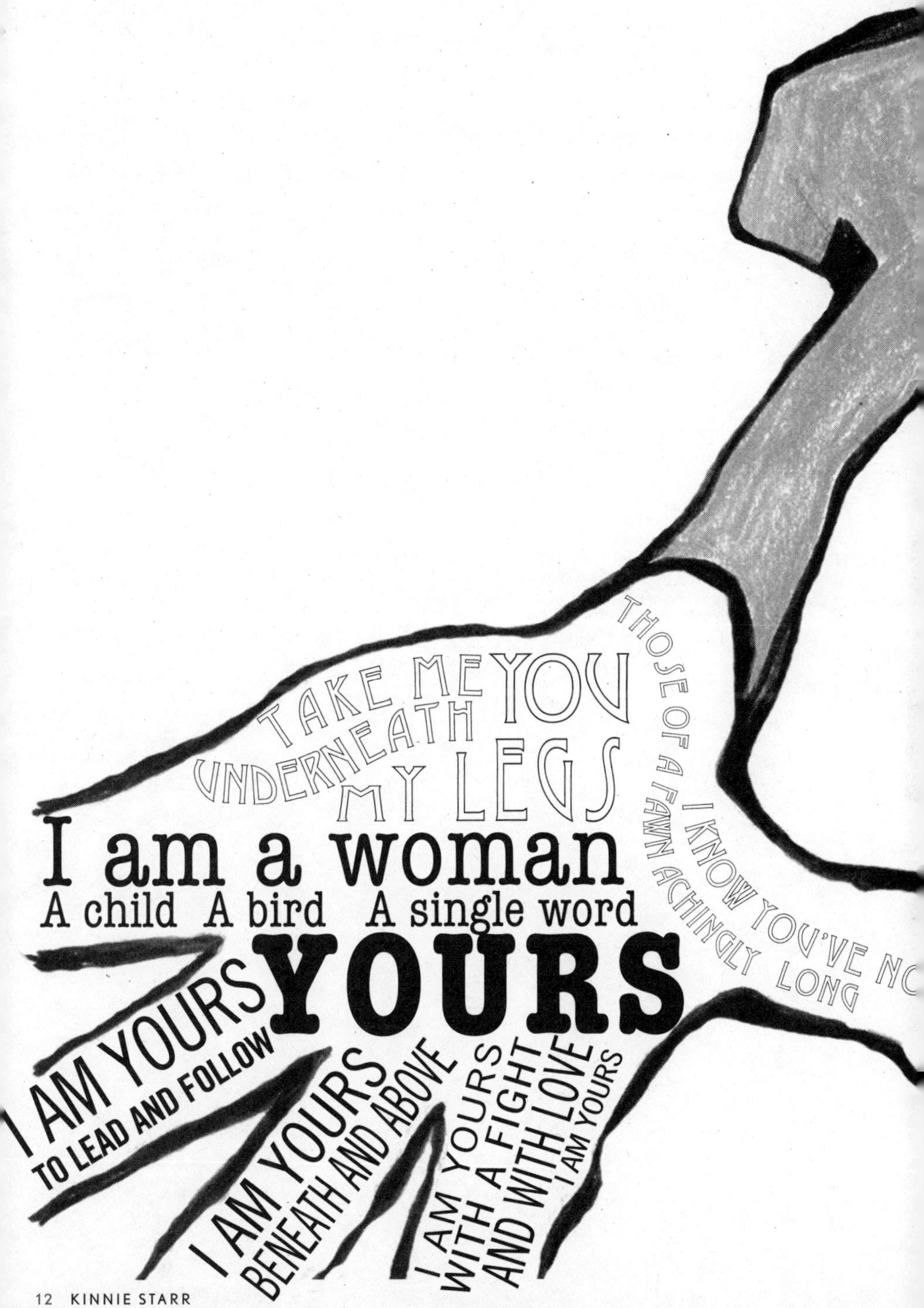
TAKE ME
YOU
UNDERNEATH
MY LEGS
THOSE OF A FAWN ACHINGLY LONG
I KNOW YOU'VE NO
I am a woman
A child A bird A single word
YOURS
I AM YOURS
TO LEAD AND FOLLOW
I AM YOURS
BENEATH AND ABOVE
I AM YOURS
WITH A FIGHT
AND WITH LOVE
I AM YOURS

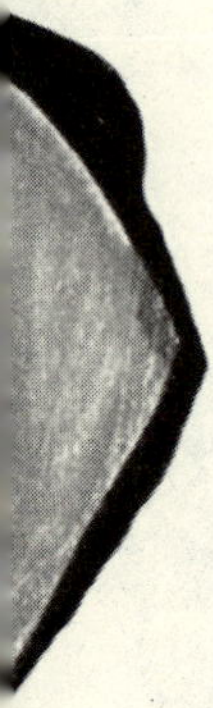

Take me
Underneath you
My legs
Those of a fawn
Achingly long
I know
You've noticed

I am a woman
A child
A bird
A single word
Yours

I am yours
To lead and follow
I am yours
Beneath and above
I am yours
With a fight
And with love
I am yours

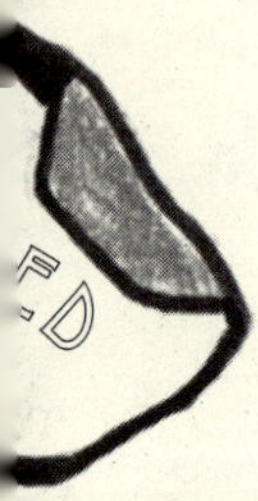

Kinnie

CROWS

THES BONES ARE ARID LIKE PRAIRIE THESE LEG

THESE ARMS ARE CHINOOK WINDS TUCKED

THESE EYES ARE CROWS CLEVER ON TELEPHONE

'E SUNRISES LONG SHAFTS OF YELLOW LIGHT

IAGONALLY INTO ANGULAR WINTER SKIES

LINES WATCHING OVER THIS LIFE

I CAN REST

I lie in your sleeping arms
Your fingers
Thread through mine
Your chest lifts
While I cry

Against my back
Your deep sighs
Wash over my fears
Your cedars
Grow round us

your moonl

ght creeps in

Your boughs
Catch cold rain
Your moonlight
Creeps in

Your birds
Fly to us
They land
Softly
Over your
Sleeping rest

Your exquisite
Arching
Rest

I WALK

FLIP ME ONTO BELLY
ONTO FIRM TABLETOP
YES THAT IS ME
THOSE
ARE
MY
AUTUMN
LEAVES

CITY LIGHTS
CROSS MY CHEST
ILLUMINATE THESE
DELICATE AND FULL
TIPPED ROSEBUD BROWN
NOBLE
HIGH
BREASTS

YOU UNLOCK
MY ORIGIN
UNKNOWN
UNKNOWN
UNKNOWN
WITH HOT SIGHS
OF IMPULSIVENESS
WE PUSH INTO
PLACES
PLACES
PLACES

Flip me onto belly
Onto firm tabletop
Yes that is me
Those are
My autumn
Leaves

City lights
Cross my chest
Illuminate these
Noble high breasts
Delicate and full
Tipped rosebud brown

You unlock
My origin
With hot sighs
Of impulsiveness
We push into
Unknown places

HAVING FULL LIPS

The lips of my face
Are like another place
Dark flower
Fruit fresh
To devour

Have the good sense
To go south
Unmeasured
Quiet
Intelligent
S L O W
Inquisitive

Now wait
With two hands beneath
Then kiss
Where lovely
These thighs meet

Paced by empathy
We share sighs
Petals bloom
You know why

You know WHY
And oh HOW
I am a lady
I flush ripe red
While we go round

SHAPED LIKE YOU

Slipped my shoes
Into your feet tonight
My type of
Holy communion

If there were God
She would be shaped
As you are now
Shirt unbuttoned
Smell of the day
Still upon you

veins • And sky water • Falling down windowpanes····I spotted two lovebirds • Kissing in an alley • I spied as their arms • Wound round each others' torsos····The night sky • Barely illuminated •
• Rhythmic • Like blood in veins • And sky water • Falling down windowpanes····I spotted two lovebirds • Kissing in an alley • I spied as their arms • Wound round each others' torsos····The nig
en • The lovers pushed forward • Rhythmic • Like blood in veins • And sky water • Falling down windowpanes····I spotted two lovebirds • Kissing in an alley • I spied as their arms • Wound roun
roken • And creek beds burst open • The lovers pushed forward • Rhythmic • Like blood in veins • And sky water • Falling down windowpanes····I spotted two lovebirds • Kissing in an alley • I sp
ween thighs····I saw creases broken • And creek beds burst open • The lovers pushed forward • Rhythmic • Like blood in veins • And sky water • Falling down windowpanes····I spotted two lov
achs • Necks • Jaws • And between thighs····I saw creases broken • And creek beds burst open • The lovers pushed forward • Rhythmic • Like blood in veins • And sky water • Falling down windo

THE LOVERS SIGHTED

rets lay • In valleys • C ... d • Rhythmic • Like blood in veins • And sky w
l themselves • Of wha ... • The lovers pushed forward • Rhythmic • Like
ered hands····They informed themselves • Of what secrets lay • In valleys • On stomachs • Necks • Jaws • And between thighs····I saw creases broken • And creek beds burst open • The lovers push
ated • The outline • Of four fevered hands····They informed themselves • Of what secrets lay • In valleys • On stomachs • Necks • Jaws • And between thighs····I saw creases broken • And creek
·The night sky • Barely illuminated • The outline • Of four fevered hands····They informed themselves • Of what secrets lay • In valleys • On stomachs • Necks • Jaws • And between thighs····I s
d round each others' torsos····The night sky • Barely illuminated • The outline • Of four fevered hands····They informed themselves • Of what secrets lay • In valleys • On stomachs • Necks • Jaw
• I spied as their arms • Wound round each others' torsos····The night sky • Barely illuminated • The outline • Of four fevered hands····They informed themselves • Of what secrets lay • In valle
wo lovebirds • Kissing in an alley • I spied as their arms • Wound round each others' torsos····The night sky • Barely illuminated • The outline • Of four fevered hands····They informed themselves
indowpanes····I spotted two lovebirds • Kissing in an alley • I spied as their arms • Wound round each others' torsos····The night sky • Barely illuminated • The outline • Of four fevered hands·
And sky water • Falling down windowpanes····I spotted two lovebirds • Kissing in an alley • I spied as their arms • Wound round each others' torsos····The night sky • Barely illuminated • The out
mic • Like blood in veins • And sky water • Falling down windowpanes····I spotted two lovebirds • Kissing in an alley • I spied as their arms • Wound round each others' torsos····The night sky • B
vers pushed forward • Rhythmic • Like blood in veins • And sky water • Falling down windowpanes····I spotted two lovebirds • Kissing in an alley • I spied as their arms • Wound round each others
eek beds burst open • The lovers pushed forward • Rhythmic • Like blood in veins • And sky water • Falling down windowpanes····I spotted two lovebirds • Kissing in an alley • I spied as their arn
·I saw creases broken • And creek beds burst open • The lovers pushed forward • Rhythmic • Like blood in veins • And sky water • Falling down windowpanes····I spotted two lovebirds • Kissing i
Jaws • And between thighs····I saw creases broken • And creek beds burst open • The lovers pushed forward • Rhythmic • Like blood in veins • And sky water • Falling down windowpanes····I spo
eys • On stomachs • Necks • Jaws • And between thighs····I saw creases broken • And creek beds burst open • The lovers pushed forward • Rhythmic • Like blood in veins • And sky water • Falling
es • Of what secrets lay • In valleys • On stomachs • Necks • Jaws • And between thighs····I saw creases broken • And creek beds burst open • The lovers pushed forward • Rhythmic • Like blood in ve
·They informed themselves • Of what secrets lay • In valleys • On stomachs • Necks • Jaws • And between thighs····I saw creases broken • And creek beds burst open • The lovers pushed forward •
line • Of four fevered hands····They informed themselves • Of what secrets lay • In valleys • On stomachs • Necks • Jaws • And between thighs····I saw creases broken • And creek beds burst open
• Barely illuminated • The outline • Of four fevered hands····They informed themselves • Of what secrets lay • In valleys • On stomachs • Necks • Jaws • And between thighs····I saw creases brok
ers' torsos····The night sky • Barely illuminated • The outline • Of four fevered hands····They informed themselves • Of what secrets lay • In valleys • On stomachs • Necks • Jaws • And between
arms • Wound round each others' torsos····The night sky • Barely illuminated • The outline • Of four fevered hands····They informed themselves • Of what secrets lay • In valleys • On stomachs
g in an alley • I spied as their arms • Wound round each others' torsos····The night sky • Barely illuminated • The outline • Of four fevered hands····They informed themselves • Of what secrets lay •
wo lovebirds • Kissing in an alley • I spied as their arms • Wound round each others' torsos····The night sky • Barely illuminated • The outline • Of four fevered hands····They informed themselves
indowpanes····I spotted two lovebirds • Kissing in an alley • I spied as their arms • Wound round each others' torsos····The night sky • Barely illuminated • The outline • Of four fevered hands·
And sky water • Falling down windowpanes····I spotted two lovebirds • Kissing in an alley • I spied as their arms • Wound round each others' torsos····The night sky • Barely illuminated • The out
mic • Like blood in veins • And sky water • Falling down windowpanes····I spotted two lovebirds • Kissing in an alley • I spied as their arms • Wound round each others' torsos····The night sky • B
vers pushed forward • Rhythmic • Like blood in veins • And sky water • Falling down windowpanes····I spotted two lovebirds • Kissing in an alley • I spied as their arms • Wound round each others
eek beds burst open • The lovers pushed forward • Rhythmic • Like blood in veins • And sky water • Falling down windowpanes····I spotted two lovebirds • Kissing in an alley • I spied as their arn
·I saw creases broken • And creek beds burst open • The lovers pushed forward • Rhythmic • Like blood in veins • And sky water • Falling down windowpanes····I spotted two lovebirds • Kissing i
Jaws • And between thighs····I saw creases broken • And creek beds burst open • The lovers pushed forward • Rhythmic • Like blood in veins • And sky water • Falling down windowpanes····I spo
eys • On stomachs • Necks • Jaws • And between thighs····I saw creases broken • And creek beds burst open • The lovers pushed forward • Rhythmic • Like blood in veins • And sky water • Falling
es • Of what secrets lay • In valleys • On stomachs • Necks • Jaws • And between thighs····I saw creases broken • And creek beds burst open • The lovers pushed forward • Rhythmic • Like blood in ve
·They informed themselves • Of what secrets lay • In valleys • On stomachs • Necks • Jaws • And between thighs····I saw creases broken • And creek beds burst open • The lovers pushed forward •
line • Of four fevered hands····They informed themselves • Of what secrets lay • In valleys • On stomachs • Necks • Jaws • And between thighs····I saw creases broken • And creek beds burst open
• Barely illuminated • The outline • Of four fevered hands····They informed themselves • Of what secrets lay • In valleys • On stomachs • Necks • Jaws • And between thighs····I saw creases brok
ers' torsos····The night sky • Barely illuminated • The outline • Of four fevered hands····They informed themselves • Of what secrets lay • In valleys • On stomachs • Necks • Jaws • And between
arms • Wound round each others' torsos····The night sky • Barely illuminated • The outline • Of four fevered hands····They informed themselves • Of what secrets lay • In valleys • On stomachs
g in an alley • I spied as their arms • Wound round each others' torsos····The night sky • Barely illuminated • The outline • Of four fevered hands····They informed themselves • Of what secrets lay •
wo lovebirds • Kissing in an alley • I spied as their arms • Wound round each others' torsos····The night sky • Barely illuminated • The outline • Of four fevered hands····They informed themselves
indowpanes····I spotted two lovebirds • Kissing in an alley • I spied as their arms • Wound round each others' torsos····The night sky • Barely illuminated • The outline • Of four fevered hands·
And sky water • Falling down windowpanes····I spotted two lovebirds • Kissing in an alley • I spied as their arms • Wound round each others' torsos····The night sky • Barely illuminated • The out
mic • Like blood in veins • And sky water • Falling down windowpanes····I spotted two lovebirds • Kissing in an alley • I spied as their arms • Wound round each others' torsos····The night sky • B
vers pushed forward • Rhythmic • Like blood in veins • And sky water • Falling down windowpanes····I spotted two lovebirds • Kissing in an alley • I spied as their arms • Wound round each others
eek beds burst open • The lovers pushed forward • Rhythmic • Like blood in veins • And sky water • Falling down windowpanes····I spotted two lovebirds • Kissing in an alley • I spied as their arn
·I saw creases broken • And creek beds burst open • The lovers pushed forward • Rhythmic • Like blood in veins • And sky water • Falling down windowpanes····I spotted two lovebirds • Kissing i
Jaws • And between thighs····I saw creases broken • And creek beds burst open • The lovers pushed forward • Rhythmic • Like blood in veins • And sky water • Falling down windowpanes····I spo
eys • On stomachs • Necks • Jaws • And between thighs····I saw creases broken • And creek beds burst open • The lovers pushed forward • Rhythmic • Like blood in veins • And sky water • Falling
es • Of what secrets lay • In valleys • On stomachs • Necks • Jaws • And between thighs····I saw creases broken • And creek beds burst open • The lovers pushed forward • Rhythmic • Like blood in ve
·They informed themselves • Of what secrets lay • In valleys • On stomachs • Necks • Jaws • And between thighs····I saw creases broken • And creek beds burst open • The lovers pushed forward •
line • Of four fevered hands····They informed themselves • Of what secrets lay • In valleys • On stomachs • Necks • Jaws • And between thighs····I saw creases broken • And creek beds burst open
• Barely illuminated • The outline • Of four fevered hands····They informed themselves • Of what secrets lay • In valleys • On stomachs • Necks • Jaws • And between thighs····I saw creases brok
ers' torsos····The night sky • Barely illuminated • The outline • Of four fevered hands····They informed themselves • Of what secrets lay • In valleys • On stomachs • Necks • Jaws • And between
arms • Wound round each others' torsos····The night sky • Barely illuminated • The outline • Of four fevered hands····They informed themselves • Of what secrets lay • In valleys • On stomachs
g in an alley • I spied as their arms • Wound round each others' torsos····The night sky • Barely illuminated • The outline • Of four fevered hands····They informed themselves • Of what secrets lay •
wo lovebirds • Kissing in an alley • I spied as their arms • Wound round each others' torsos····The night sky • Barely illuminated • The outline • Of four fevered hands····They informed themselves
indowpanes····I spotted two lovebirds • Kissing in an alley • I spied as their arms • Wound round each others' torsos····The night sky • Barely illuminated • The outline • Of four fevered hands·
And sky water • Falling down windowpanes····I spotted two lovebirds • Kissing in an alley • I spied as their arms • Wound round each others' torsos····The night sky • Barely illuminated • The out
mic • Like blood in veins • And sky water • Falling down windowpanes····I spotted two lovebirds • Kissing in an alley • I spied as their arms • Wound round each others' torsos····The night sky • B
vers pushed forward • Rhythmic • Like blood in veins • And sky water • Falling down windowpanes····I spotted two lovebirds • Kissing in an alley • I spied as their arms • Wound round each others
eek beds burst open • The lovers pushed forward • Rhythmic • Like blood in veins • And sky water • Falling down windowpanes····I spotted two lovebirds • Kissing in an alley • I spied as their arn
·I saw creases broken • And creek beds burst open • The lovers pushed forward • Rhythmic • Like blood in veins • And sky water • Falling down windowpanes····I spotted two lovebirds • Kissing i
Jaws • And between thighs····I saw creases broken • And creek beds burst open • The lovers pushed forward • Rhythmic • Like blood in veins • And sky water • Falling down windowpanes····I spo
eys • On stomachs • Necks • Jaws • And between thighs····I saw creases broken • And creek beds burst open • The lovers pushed forward • Rhythmic • Like blood in veins • And sky water • Falling
es • Of what secrets lay • In valleys • On stomachs • Necks • Jaws • And between thighs····I saw creases broken • And creek beds burst open • The lovers pushed forward • Rhythmic • Like blood in ve
·They informed themselves • Of what secrets lay • In valleys • On stomachs • Necks • Jaws • And between thighs····I saw creases broken • And creek beds burst open • The lovers pushed forward •
line • Of four fevered hands····They informed themselves • Of what secrets lay • In valleys • On stomachs • Necks • Jaws • And between thighs····I saw creases broken • And creek beds burst open
• Barely illuminated • The outline • Of four fevered hands····They informed themselves • Of what secrets lay • In valleys • On stomachs • Necks • Jaws • And between thighs····I saw creases brok
ers' torsos····The night sky • Barely illuminated • The outline • Of four fevered hands····They informed themselves • Of what secrets lay • In valleys • On stomachs • Necks • Jaws • And between
arms • Wound round each others' torsos····The night sky • Barely illuminated • The outline • Of four fevered hands····They informed themselves • Of what secrets lay • In valleys • On stomachs
g in an alley • I spied as their arms • Wound round each others' torsos····The night sky • Barely illuminated • The outline • Of four fevered hands····They informed themselves • Of what secrets lay •
wo lovebirds • Kissing in an alley • I spied as their arms • Wound round each others' torsos····The night sky • Barely illuminated • The outline • Of four fevered hands····They informed themselves
indowpanes····I spotted two lovebirds • Kissing in an alley • I spied as their arms • Wound round each others' torsos····The night sky • Barely illuminated • The outline • Of four fevered hands·
And sky water • Falling down windowpanes····I spotted two lovebirds • Kissing in an alley • I spied as their arms • Wound round each others' torsos····The night sky • Barely illuminated • The out
mic • Like blood in veins • And sky water • Falling down windowpanes····I spotted two lovebirds • Kissing in an alley • I spied as their arms • Wound round each others' torsos····The night sky • B

I spotted two lovebirds
Kissing in an alley
I spied as their arms
Wound round each others' torsos

The night sky
Barely illuminated
The outline
Of four fevered hands

They informed themselves
Of what secrets lay
In valleys
On stomachs
Necks
Jaws
And between thighs

I saw creases broken
And creek beds burst open
The lovers pushed forward
Rhythmic
Like blood in veins
And sky water
Falling down windowpanes

I LEARNED TO RUN

Hands loose
In half-fists
Falling
I learned to run
This year
From holding
Onto nothing!

I carved greater range
Into my heart's
Perimeter
I broadened
My tiny *Circumference*

HOW LONG WILL

I swung keen
These bony arms
With their
Very own charm

I hung frail
These deer legs
Elegant
From this ribcage

THIS TAKE?

I dug in
These thin feet
Heels down
Into
Shaky ground

My feet pounded the earth
I kicked up dirt
Rocks
Ice
Bits of cedar

Combed my face

One step
Two step
Three step
Four
Five
For the way my dad
Used to chide me
Ride me
Until the room
Split with laughter

Like a good
Half-breed father
He made fun
Of his *Funny looking daughter*

FOR THE MOST MAGNIFICENT

Skin and bones
And even back then
I preferred
Being alone

HEARTBREAK

Six
S E V E N
Eight
For the most
Magnificent
Heartbreak

For the way
He paraded her
Round the city
Knowing
How best *To derail me*

Nine
Ten
Eleven
Twelve

Thirteen
For my mom's birth date
Lucky thirteen
To be born of her

Fourteen
Fifteen
Sixteen
Seventeen

HOW LONG will this take?

I DID MY

Eighteen
Nineteen
Twenty

Twenty steps
I see my breath
Twenty steps
I passed the test
Twenty steps
I learned to run
I learned to run

BEST

I did my best

RIFLES

I speak of a private need
To feel part of a shifting public
To be seen by other brown eyes
Sometimes blue or grey or green
Eyes that are slowly taking back
What was
And is
At the root
Of what always has been

I am because I have come to be
Unformed braids
Hit my shoulders awkwardly
Half-formed opinions
Half-bred blood and DNA

I am because I have come to be
Both limited and expansive
I draw on resources
Of ancestors misunderstood
And the profound desire to CHANGE
Re-emerge into my true self

I speak because I am spoken to
By my grandfather's graceful hands
A rifle and a nation
With no place to stand

FENCES

Father speaks of red

Auntie speaks
of white

Both stories get told

By the table

On the

Same night

FATHER SPEAKS OF RED

Auntie speaks of white

Both stories get told · By the table

On the · Same night

BOTH SIDES CAN BE LIES

Both sides can be lies
Both be truthful
and right
Just depends
Which side
Of the fence
Is used for sight

Both sides can be lies
Both be truthful and right
Just depends
Which side
Of the fence
Is used for sight

LESSER THINGS

LEGS AND WINGS AND FEATHERS
AND TO KNOW YOU KNOW YOUR
OWN HEART
THIS EARTH KNOWS WINGS AND
FEATHERS
AND WITH SEED AND SOIL DOES
GIVE US START

OUR SHOULDERS DRAG
FROM THE TIRED BIRD WINGS
WE HIDE

AND THIS IS THE BEAUTY
OF OUR BEING
AND THE BEAUTY OF
LESSER THINGS

LEGS AND WINGS AND FEATHERS
AND TO KNOW YOU KNOW YOUR
OWN HEART
THIS EARTH KNOWS WINGS AND
FEATHERS
AND WITH SEED AND SOIL DOES
GIVE US START

OUR SHOULDERS DRAG
FROM THE TIRED BIRD WINGS
WE HIDE

AND THIS IS THE BEAUTY
OF OUR BEING
AND THE BEAUTY OF
LESSER THINGS

THIS IS NOT MY TIME

My feet are not

From here
Blood boiling
From centuries passed

The building signs have not yet sprung up
And residential housing has not yet
Positioned itself
On lawns
Where we leave toys
Fridges

Fishnets
And old cars

Come to my time
Where fabric falls
On the female frame
With ease and grace

Silk
Heavy cottons
Linen
Hand-sewn lace

Where water heats more slowly
On gas stoves
And bedtime fires are set
Each morning before sunrise

BEIGE

BEIGE IS THE COLOR
OF THE NEXT STAGE
WE CAN CLEAN THE "ISMS"
AND FLUSH OUT RAGE

LET US HEIGHTEN SIGHT
LET US LIGHTEN LIGHT
STRENGTHEN UNISON
TWO-THOUSAND FLIGHTS

WE ARE NOT WATERTIGHT
NO, WE BLEND LIKE THE RAIN
AND WE UNIFY TO BREAK OUT
THE SEASONS AGAIN

POOR JUDGMENT
COMES FROM POOR SIGHT
WE MUST SEARCH
THE DEAD OF NIGHT
FOR MOONLIGHT

THAT SHINES FROM US ALL
AS WE GATHER AND IGNITE
IN THE BLACKEST OF HEMATITE
THERE IS STILL WHITE

KINNIE

PONY

Now snow falls and dreamtime calls
And I'm with a sweaty mare in a dusty stall
Her skin is hot; she breathes fresh air
From her nostrils exhalation of despair

We ran in a field I upon her back
Picking up speed we were picking up slack
Heels kick up speed picks up
Like a long espresso in a clay cup

And we were braced without a trace of hesitation
Ran like Columbus annihilated nations
Ran like the US should have
Left alone the Haitians

Yes we ran across a very long field
I gripped her hard in her flanks with my heels
I held her mane and at times held her neck
Upon her back I was nothing but a speck
Of dust and I trusted her with my well-being
Preadolescent child not yet seeing

I saw nothing but the wind past my eyes
Gripped the sweaty mare and to my surprise
Well I found myself falling like time was stalling
Wondering how long it would take to hit the ground
Wondering how many bones would break
And what would be the sound

But I just kind of thumped
And the field felt soft
Rolled around for a bit
Feeling dizzy and lost
And far away was that sweaty mare
She left me on my nerdy ass
Left me to stare
At the dust at her heels
And how it did feel
To know I can never tame another being
And that's just the deal

TAKE FLIGHT

I saw an eagle
Take flight the other day
And all my "Indian" stereotypes
Got in the way

He was just feathers
And strength
And movement on treetops
The gulls heckled him
Unwilling to stop

An eagle is not
Such an unlikely sight
But I twist
Round conditioning
Caught up in his flight

Is it my red DNA
That sends shivers down my spine?
Or my fair side that loves
And learns equally with time?

I try not to name
My blood dilution
I can't separate
That's not part of the solution

Blood is a debate
Of human abstraction
Not to be mistaken
For some
Vague indication
Of my skeleton's
Lack of perfection

I am of the earth
Rocks moved by friction
Dug up and dumped on
By needless ambition

Tightening and brightening
The new generation
Governed by my blood's
Blinding devotion

To the beat
To the bass
To never getting
In the chase

To never getting
In the race
That could take me
From you

So feel free
To look upon me
As what you
Choose to see

I am fairness
In the winter
I am brown
Like summer's father

All my blood
Knows the earth
Is the mother
I wake some nights
To see the moon
Ache with wonder
At my family truths
Buried stale under

I look upon
My father's face
I see the sorry
In his race
I see
The swollen
Way he stands
See the bottle
In his
Shaking hand

But MILLIONS of him
Built this land
CITIES of his
Calloused hands

Doctors
Lawyers
Preachers
Teachers
Workers
Of the heart
And mind

But that "Indian" stereotype
Paints a vision less kind
That's why the eagle
In the sky
Is watching
As we change
Our minds

ALL MY BLO

KNOWS THE EA

IS THE M

I WAKE SOME NIG

TO SEE THE M

ACHE WITH

AT MY FAMILY TRUTH

BURIED STALE

OD

TH

OTHER

TS

ON

ONDER

ER

CASTLEGAR

That full moon
Held all sides of you
Eyes and mouth
Close to mine
Your face lit
By quiet streets

Our hands
Are and were
As they should be
Incantations of praise
Stroking plains

Shoulders
Arms
Breasts
Thighs

Up this close
You are
More impassioned
Than I had
Best imagined

Fine mouth
Set on sleep
And stun
In the same
Heaving moment

I was loos

I was loosened
Those hands
Pulled me down
My sides
And centre
Fell out of me

ned

My arms became
The busted roots

Of a cedar
Too thin

Eyes

The muscles
Across my heart
Were too
Weakly bound

In one easy step
I was stripped

Eyes drawn bare

Of green
Gold
Brown

rawn bare

I WAS ALONE

Distance
Laziness
And petulance
Unwound us

He turned
On his splintered axis
Bent and broken
Toward her

I found
A bear
Waiting

In his forest
For me

I turned
To the moon
I grew

Into a tree

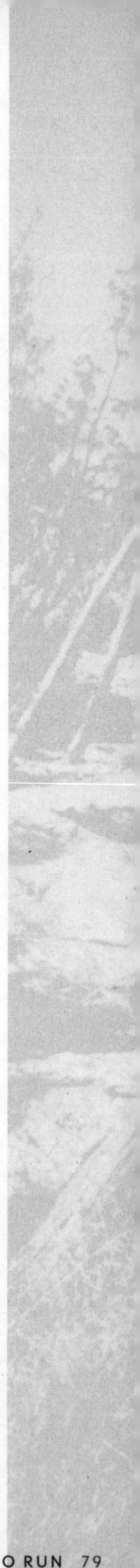

I Turned
To the moon
I grew

Into a Tree

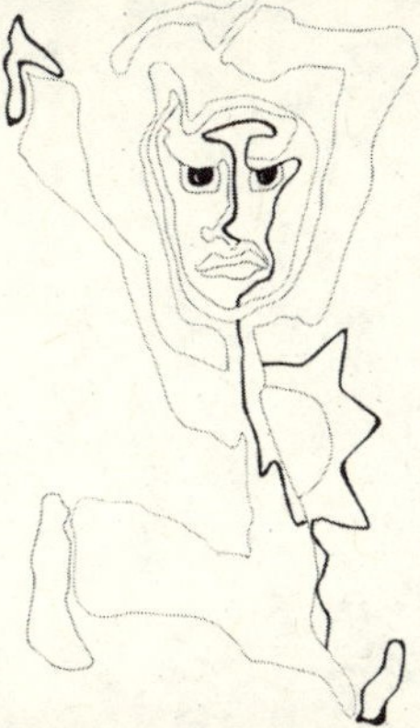

BED

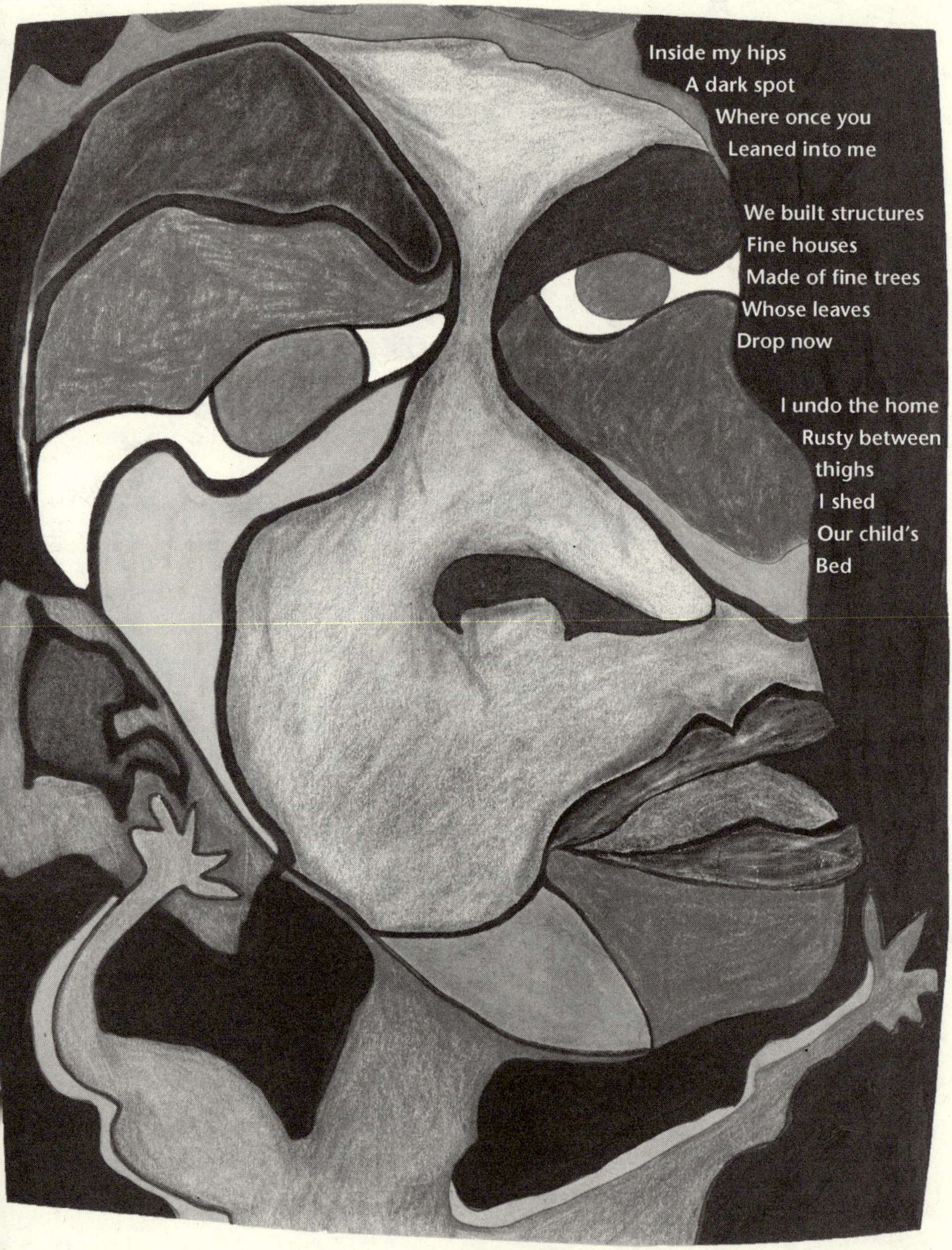

Inside my hips
A dark spot
Where once you
Leaned into me

We built structures
Fine houses
Made of fine trees
Whose leaves
Drop now

I undo the home
Rusty between
thighs
I shed
Our child's
Bed

TOOLS

I don't know how to love • Wasn't given the tools • At least not the right ones • Maybe some dress shirts • Worn loose and open • Ill-fitting • On whoever wore them

A spoon to write w

ork to read letters • A saucepan to carve • Holes in the side • Of a mountain • A book • To bash away • Bad dreams

THE USUAL ENDS

EXHAUSTION
HAS HIT OUR COMMUNITY
LOW EMPTINESS
WEIGHS CHINS DOWN
THEY SCRAPE PAVEMENT
WE DRAG OURSELVES
THROUGH EMPTY ENTERTAINMENT

WE DRI
THRO
INTO P
and BORED G
BARE BO
THA
•••THE USU

HALF ASLEEP
GH *our* LIVES
RNOGRAPHY
S

ING TITS
PROMISE
ENDS...

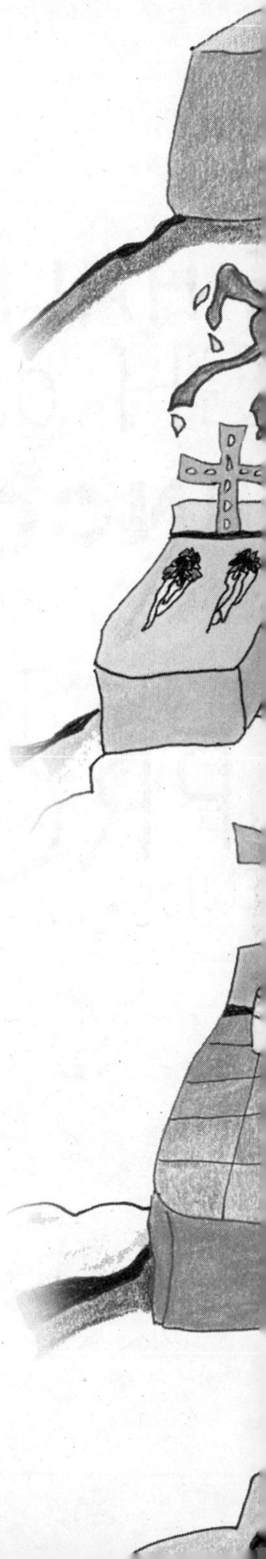

LOONS CALL

FORLORN TALES
LYRICAL AND WILD
Low antique songs
Cross great lakes
Guess the old ones
Are still awake

MOON RISES

TREES LINED BLACK
Become grey
And are at last
Slate-green

NIGHTTIME

SETTLES IN
And winds
Push spirits 'round
Like playing cards

ABOUT THE AUTHOR

Kinnie Starr began making her presence felt around 1995 with edgy visual arts, graffiti, rhymes, outspoken race and gender politics, decidedly unorthodox performances, stunning good looks and envelope-pushing, beat-slamming recordings. This combination earned her a well-deserved and devoted fan base, a record contract with Mercury/Island/DefJam (1996–1999), and an immediate connection with critics and consumers alike.

In 2003 she sung and cat walked in Las Vegas for Cirque du Soleil's sexy x-rated show, Zumanity and that same

year was nominated in Canada for a Juno as Best New Artist. Since then she has played the National Aboriginal Achievement Awards twice and written music for Zellers, the *L-Word* and the feature movie *Thirteen.*

Starr teaches with Artstarts In Schools (BC) and the Manitoba Audio Recording Industry Association. She is also the co-founder of Vancouver's Aboriginal Music Lab, a weeklong intensive for emerging native artists seeking international level performance and recording skills.

After four albums and a decade of successful international touring, *How I Learned to Run* is Starr's first book of poetry and drawings. It is a contemplative look at love, history, sex and the complexities of being part Mohawk in a Canadian family that has yet to come to terms with its indigenous roots.

ABOUT HOUSE OF PARLANCE

House of Parlance is a new media company and trade book publisher inspired by literary and visual storytelling. We work with authors, writers, artists, illustrators and spoken word poets. From high-quality titles to electronic media, our works promote new connections between artists, authors, and their worldwide audiences.

We find emerging talent from the 21st century's richest and most potent creative incubator: Everywhere. We're currently working on several new titles for kids, adults and everyone in between. We will also publish some fresh poetry and spoken word titles from some of the finest voices out there.

Check out our website at www.houseofparlance.com

house of parlance
media inc.

ADDITIONAL TITLES FROM HOUSE OF PARLANCE MEDIA:

Stickboy (August 2008) by Shane Koyczan
Visiting Hours (2005) by Shane Koyczan

Please visit our website (www.houseofparlance.com) for more information on these titles and authors.

PHOTO CREDITS

All photos by Alida Kinnie Starr except:

Page 31: Alida Kinnie Starr, Donna Starr, and unidentified friend
Photo by Michael Starr

Page 48: Alida Kinnie Starr, Michael Starr, Russell Starr
Photo by Donna Starr

Page 64: Chris Starr and Alida Kinnie Starr
Photo by Michael Starr

Page 65: Alida Kinnie Starr
Photo by Donna Starr

HOW I LEARNED TO R